Light Hearted
POEMS
Looking for
HOMES

BOB MCCLUSKEY

LIGHT HEARTED POEMS LOOKING FOR HOMES

Thanks to Sunshine Hills Foursquare Church (6749 120th Street, Delta, BC V4E 2A7, Phone 604-594-0810, Fax 604-594-6673) for all of their help and support with my books.

Printed in Canada

ISBN: 978-1-4866-1100-3

Word Alive Press
131 Cordite Road, Winnipeg, MB R3W 1S1
www.wordalivepress.ca

MIX
Paper from
responsible sources
FSC
www.fsc.org   FSC® C016245

Cataloguing in Publication may be obtained through Library and Archives Canada

Dedication

The time has arrived when my persistently accumulating poetry must see the light of day and so, another book...Hopefully, time and experience have added somewhat to my poetic skills, but only you readers can be the judge of this, and so I beg your indulgence once more...My bride's family as well as my own plus many assorted friends, have been welcome grist for my poetic mill and my sincere hope is that I have caused no offence to any and with that hope, I dedicate this book to them all.

Introduction

Why another book, or more specifically, why this book? Well, why not......and,since poetry doth ever flow, I have gathered this collection, worthy of thy kind inspection, it doth ever seem to grow. Wherever it doth come from, it cometh not from dereliction, since I'm free from that affliction, I just honestly don't know. Some of it speaks Godly virtue; I assure you it won't say anything to ever hurt you, as you read along the way. Other parts portray my humor, I have even heard the rumor these might tickle the consumer, but that's not for me to say. I assure you if you buy it, you will suffer no dismay. Just relax awhile and try it, I would never ever lie, it at least might keep thee quiet, thy confreres wouldst ne'er deny it would be to them, a blessing on life's way.

HEY, I KNOW YOU
May 19, 2015.

Hey, I know you
Oh no you don't
You only know what you can see
But tho you look real hard, you won't
See me

What you observe's the vehicle
That carries me around
I'm on the inside hiding out
I weigh an ounce or thereabout
My vehicle, about 200 pound

My vehicle takes all the praise
'cause that's all you can see
I sit inside with eyes aglaze
Pretending I'm not there, most days
Whilst he pretends he's me.

But one day I will fly the coop
From flesh I'm gonna flee
You'll see me lying in a bier
Oh no you won't, 'cause I aint here
You're looking at my vehicle
But that aint me

WHO ARE WE

May 22, 2015

Who are we, travelin' along,
We are brothers and sisters, I guess.
You ask, "How do you know",
why, you just have to go
to the Bible to feel truth's caress.

It all started with Adam and Eve,
God gave Adam a wife to relieve
Adam's feelings of angst,
did God get any thanks
when He caused Adam's wife to conceive.

Well, the proof's in the puddin' they say,
her first son received the name Cain.
Eve's behaviour, tho bland
became quite out of hand,
Eve was caught raising Cain every day

Their next son received the name Abel,
that name didst great promise portend.
But then Cain didst erase
a fourth of the whole race,
when he killed his own bro' in the end.

So who are we, I asked at the start,
the answer seems evident now.
Because Satan snuck in,
brother Cain didst begin
the deception in each human heart.

ARTIFICIAL INTELLIGENCE
May 16, 2015

I am slowly becoming aware as I read
of bodies of very intelligent men, who try
to follow a goal to succeed
in developing artificial intelligence, then
loosely designated A.I.

They refer to time's laps from fish to monkeys,
then the time lapse from monkeys to you and me.
But prospects of success are doomed from the part
where they speculate that man had his start
as a monkey, a premise that never could be.

They believe they're part of the next major event
in the evolutionary process of man.
They believe they can create a thinking machine,
self reliant, self aware, why, it might even dream,
just picture this world if you can.

I imagine psychiatrists, with hordes of machines
lining up at their office doors.
Exercised by psychoses, inflicted when
boss machines cruelly embarrassed them,
by suggesting they wash the floors.

BOB MCCLUSKEY

Or I see machines chasing women because
they were programmed to fall in love.
More psychoses when after the women were found,
machines wheels went in circles, around and round,
while God's laughing in heaven above.

God created man's mind to be able to think,
with a brain that's a marvel to see.
It can't be imitated, that's far too overrated,
God placed man at the head when created,
that's how it forever will be.

WRETCHED MAN THAT I AM

May 15, 2015

God says that when the Gentiles
who do not have the law, do by nature
the things if the law, they show the law
written in their hearts in the day
when God shall judge the secrets of men.

For which this Gentile says, Thank God!
Wash me Oh God, in the precious Blood
of Jesus Christ and cleanse me
from all unrighteousness, for I am a sinful man.

For the good that I would I do not:
but the evil I would not do, that I do.
I do however, delight in the law of God
after the inward man.

But I see another law in my members,
warring after the law of my mind,
bringing me into captivity
to the law of sin in my members.

Oh wretched man that I am,
who shall deliver me from the body of this death.
I thank God through Jesus Christ our Lord
that there is now no condemnation
to them which are in Christ Jesus.
Who walk not after the flesh but after the Spirit.

6

For the law of the Spirit of life in Christ Jesus
hath made me free from the law of sin and death.
To which every Born Again Christian saith, Amen!

I DON'T HAVE TIME

May 14, 2015

"I don't have time"
Oh yes you do, we all have time
The same amount, at least until
By God's design
Our time stands still

"I don't have time"
Why not, did you lose it
You must have time
You can't refuse it, at least until
Your time stands still

"I don't have time"
Well, if I could I would
Give you some of mine
If we only understood
Before our time stands still

"I don't have time"
Well, that's too bad
God has a sweet design
To give you lots of time
In His eternity

BOB MCCLUSKEY

"I don't have time"
Ask God for some
He travels in and out of time
To fashion His Divine
Design for everyone
Until our end of time

INVISIBLE WORLDS

May 12, 2015

The world is so huge, yet the world is so small,
creation unfolds far beyond our eye.
We cannot penetrate far into the sky,
to the place where God started it all.

Oh, we are seeing farther and farther no doubt,
as we orbit our telescopes up and about.
But as far as we go, we cannot ever know,
all the grandeur revealed in God's heavenly glow.

So inquisitive man, come back down to earth,
turn your telescopes around, your vision inverse.
See the worlds that flourish right under your feet,
for the needs they have, their worlds are complete

Mites so very small, they're unseen to our eye,
yet some live on eyelashes, leading me to ask why,
God didst ever create these invisible worlds,
our electron microscopes now can espy.

Worlds of mites crawling on us, we can't even feel,
spider web one hundred times thinner than hair.
Yet weight for weight, much stronger than steel,
bacteria even ten times as small, live there.

Near those bacteria, virus ten times smaller still,
with yet smaller, three strands of minute D.N.A.
And these numberless hordes all exist, if you will,
to live and to die in God's world every day.

So much man has learned as his knowledge has grown,
there must be a purpose for these creatures to be.
God has opened some treasures, the rest we will see
in heaven, when we'll know even as we are known.

LOST MINDS

May 7, 2015

Move invisibly,
thru a madhouse melange
of unfortunate,
mindless lost souls looking strange.
Necessity requires,
freedom must be restrained,
not against their will,
for their will has decayed
as their actions portrayed.

But if eyes were provided
by God, to reveal
Satan's evil world,
where demons are real.
We'd see who's really keeping
Many of these lost souls.
We'd see demons creeping,
or delightedly leaping,
torturing, steering,
with demonic leering
the confusion and fearing
most mad men uphold.

This applies not to all,
but to many, I feel.
After mankind didst fall,
Satan managed to steal

BOB MCCLUSKEY

God's free will from some
who didst lean to his lies.
Some would later become
lost minds we wouldst reprise
if we could, but we can't.
God alone be their judge,
I thank God its not men,
for men carry a grudge
and are blinded when
they see no sin in themselves.

GOD MADE WOMAN

May 8, 2015

God formed man from the dust of the earth,
then removed man's rib from over his heart.
With it God fashioned woman for man,
to complement man right from the start.

To man's aggression, woman tempered compassion,
for man's lust she emblazoned love.
To man's strength, woman added persuasion,
when God gave her a heart like a dove.

For impatience, she highlights long suffering,
to man's violence, she offereth peace.
From man's hairy face, God's commanding grace
formed her beauty, to nevermore cease.

God looked on creation, on woman and man,
God saw it was good, took His rest.
He had tempered man, as only God can,
with female introspection, according to plan,
as man's survival doth keenly attest.

So remember Oh man, God made you the head
to prefer one another, to bless.
You'll have great peace in life, if you value your wife,
God designed female wisdom, to save you from strife,
when He meld you together, one flesh.

GOD'S IMITATORS
May 6, 2015

Have you noticed, God has lots of imitators,
who strive to stay aloof, above the crowd.
They ration what they say,
as God, they have to be that way,
can't run off at the mouth, that's not allowed.

Their gaze stays just a little elevated,
as they concentrate on things we cannot see.
God must be quite blasé,
at least they portray God that way,
as they deign to judge the likes of you and me.

Their own conduct is of course, quite unimpeachable,
as becometh one who never makes mistakes.
God looks on us from above,
His imitators, God must love,
for He taught me to repent, for heaven's sake!

BROAD THE WAY
TO DESTRUCTION

May 6, 2015

At some point in life, shouldst man e'er decide
to lift up his eyes from the dirt.
What might he espy on his wayward path,
that could possibly be to his hurt.

Perhaps he might see, something wherewith he
could profit withal, a surprise.
At the road's divide, ahead he must decide
twixt two gates, one destructive, one wise.

The gate on his right seemeth narrow and strait,
he had baggage which could not fit thru.
Heavy baggage he'd carried for most of his life,
he just could not discard nor eschew.

On his left, a wide gate he could negotiate,
with all of his baggage as well.
But not far down that road, the devil's abode
waits, to introduce him to hell.

He then saw a great light, in the midst of his plight,
a voice asked, whom serve you this day.
He fell flat on his face, embraced Jesus sweet grace,
and threw all his old baggage away.

BOB McCLUSKEY

HOW COULD THEY KNOW
May 5, 2015

There's a mystery for which I cannot account,
which puzzles this old guy no end.
As each physical problem in turn I surmount,
T.V. makes it a major event.

Each affliction in turn, as my functions decline
seems to grace the whole country enmasse.
They'd advertise cures for each hurt, just in time,
thank God my problem's not gas.

I could share in detail each affliction I'm in,
to suffice, I'll just give you the list.
Joint pain, psoriasis, E.D., itchy skin,
and a last one that today, joined the list.

You can guess my surprise, before my very eyes,
on T.V., a fake doctor didst say.
That he had the cure for all tingling feet,
the same thing I incurred just today.

How could he have known, we've been here alone,
and I've hardly begun to complain.
They have spies everywhere; I must now wash my hair,
dandruff might start him selling again.

THE MIRACLE WOMB

May 3, 2015

God's creation amazes, consider the womb,
woman is designed every month, to abound.
Deep down unseen, there's a miracle soon,
as an egg is formed, an egg which contains
all the elements required to create a man,
all that is, with two major exceptions.
First, a spark is required before life can be found,
then a male is required to deposit a seed
for the egg to be granted all she will need,
no deletion.

But let's stop for a moment, life's so easy to say,
but consider the miracle of love underway.
Way inside, in the dark, out of everyone's sight,
who's assembling those myriad parts.
God designed us! God spoke and we came to light
when He fashioned the noses, the fingers and hearts
in secretion.

And another expression of love do I see,
you will note I referred to the egg as she.
For the egg manifests that sweet womanly part,
that displays in the act of the egg from the start.
She opens her arms to the seed's penetrate
and envelopes her lover completely within.
When this love she doth state, God can inaugurate
love's completion.

BOB McCLUSKEY

VOCABULARY LACKING
May 2, 2015

The language of some young folk,
on my middle aged ear,
no understanding doth evoke
in older listeners, I fear.
With guttural expressions
of agreement or dissent,
one wonders, mystified
where their vocabulary went.

Tho I hope their speak is English,
their expression doth extinguish
any hope we might commune
with some intelligence, I fear.
Their speech, guttural and boorish,
sounds somewhat like modern Moorish,
are they cursing when conversing,
that could be what I hear.

If they'd elucidate distinctly,
'twould encourage us to think we
might share a single language
that's yet thankfully extant.
But after years and years of trying,
I fear all hope is dying,
that we'll dialogue together,
that's the finish of my rant.

WHITE KNUCKLED

May 2, 2015

Long life upon reflection,
doth necessitate
a constant need
for man to guard his heart.
For therein wickedness
doth careless, percolate,
whilst lack of spiritual
guidance at life's start,
leaves open wound
where Satan plays his part.

Ignorance shall ne'er
instruct forgiveness,
whilst white knuckled,
holding judgement's rail.
The time God calleth man
to plead repentance,
to open up heart's door,
give Jesus entrance,
is when he's still alive,
tho in travail.

BOB MCCLUSKEY

God revealeth right and wrong
to every sinner,
all creation blazons forth
Creator's truth.
God's Holy Spirit
speaks to hearts,
that's where God's
revelation starts,
that's where men
choose their eternity, forsooth.

MY D.N.A.

May 2, 2015

When I take the deep six someday,
what becomes of my D.N.A.
Will God record my codes
ere my essence erodes,
and my double helix fades away.

No one's D.N.A. matches mine,
at least none I've been able to see.
That sweet twisting coil,
is made up just to foil
any rascal from replacing me.

So, when I've at last gone away,
taking with me, demeanor placid.
I'll remove every gene,
non could ever demean
my unique nucleic acid.

If some rascal tries taking my place,
declaring he's me, that he's Bob.
Just check his D.N.A.,
his chromosomes will betray,
that it's me he is trying to rob.

BOB MCCLUSKEY

BE LOVED
May 2, 2015

Why do we strive
All the days we're alive
To be loved
You know I'm not wrong
We're all trippin' along
I aint talkin' no jive
This is where we belong
Lay on me a high five
We all sing the same song
So dispel that disguise
And be loved

The first step I'm told
Before we're too old
Is to first love our self
Before anyone else
We then can obey
What God had to say
Love neighbor as self
Then you'll
Have a good day
By the way

HIS GOOSE IS COOKED

May 1, 2015

I've incurred much abuse
All because of my muse
Yet its really not me
Writing poetry
It must be my muse
At least that's my excuse
I don't call
He arrives
If I fall
He survives
I do find him at times
Quite obtuse
Tho I hide behind blinds
What's the use
He does help me
With rhymes
But I'm tempted betimes
To microwave
His insatiable goose

POLICE ON STRIKE
May 1, 2015

There's a manifestation of late,
in American cities, of pent up hate.
Manifest by some blacks, leading up to attacks
on police, on authority.

Everyone understands persecution,
in police, there undoubtedly be
some who hate blacks, with unfair attacks
on their rights, on their liberty.

But response is wrong, an unmanageable throng
is now burning and looting enmasse.
In their own neighbourhood, without any restraint
they're destroying as if justified, which they aint,
they'll soon call them the homeless class.

I even heard men there, loudly declare
that to Christian beliefs they adhere.
But the picture I see as they burn and smash,
does not reflect love Jesus taught us, alas,
repentant tears in the morning will sear.

We had better beware how we treat the police,
they're not perfect, but they're all we've got.
Montreal Police went on strike, to Satan's delight,
criminals without Cops, crawling from under rocks
ran amuck in that town, day and night.

HOW DOTH RAIN SUSPEND

April 30, 2015

There be mysteries evolution can't explain,
for instance rain. You answer technically,
but will you please explain to me,
how doth suspension of those lakes on high,
sustain.

Like yesterday, it rained all day, engaging
us in buckets of wet souvenirs of Jesus Love.
How doth mass suspension high above,
presage final release, when time to rain
again.

Or take butterflies!
At certain times of year, they go
to wintering grounds down south, below,
where each one propagates, then dies.
I've never heard them telling lies,
so how could they explain.

How can their children, ever know
of northern lands where ice and snow
has melted so they now can go.
Their parents could not tell them...so
its God they entertain.

BOB MCCLUSKEY

More grand examples might I give
if I could think; right off the top
just for this poem , that's all I've got.
But that's enough, to help you live
eternal life with Jesus Christ,
in heaven to remain.

SO YOU EXIST, RIGHT

April 30, 2015

So, you exist, right!
Of course you exist, you can always tell
By the pain you suffered that time you fell
And broke your wrist, so all is well
God gave you two, assuming of course
That there is a God

Or even worse
You just occurred, descended from apes
Just as easily could have come from snakes
Or even a bird, but that's absurd
You're too heavy to fly, I guess that's why
No flocks of people inhabit the sky

But you wouldn't be people
You'd be what they call avian
Not Middle Eastern and not Scandinavian
You might even end up a quadruped
In which case you could run at terrific speed
And a nice feather bed, you'd no longer need

BOB MCCLUSKEY

But I think we must end this conjecture right here
If there were no people, there'd be no beer
Then what would alcoholics drink
You can see my logic is indisputable
God gave you a brain and taught you to think
The existence of God is absolutable
Tho most of the time, I find God inscrutable

POETICAL INSIGHT

May 1, 2015

What is this inner urge all about,
this unformed expression of need.
To give voice, to express
that these poems, at a guess
are decreed.

It riseth up from somewhere inside,
to struggle and strive for release.
Deep down somewhere hidden,
making entrance unbidden,
until answered, refuseth to cease.

So you have to believe, its not me
that decreed, that decided it had to be.
It took over my head,
comes unbidden to bed,
even wakes when I go for a pee.

But it isn't all bad, there is joy to be had,
regaling my sweetheart each day.
God gave me this gift
just to give her a lift,
that is what I suspect God might say.

TIMES PASSAGING

April 29, 2015

Where hast thou flown
sweet youth.
It seemeth only yesteryear
I spent thee carelessly, forsooth.
indifferent to time's passaging,
blind to redemption's truth.

Time's passaging, man decadent
regardeth not.
Doth airily dispel said time
pursuing Sue or Clementine,
unmindful where those moments went
now oh, so vainly sought.

If grieving Christ, we now could see
whilst in our sin, we bask.
Our suffering then wouldst needless be,
for Jesus paid the price when He
died just for us, for you and me,
we only have to ask.

YON GOLDEN SUN
April 28, 2015

Yon golden sun, rules well the day
ere twilight's sweet enthralling.
Then dissipating, fades away
to starlight's raptured calling.

No longer shall her golden way,
vast heaven's vaults, illuminate.
Whilst stars in solemn light array,
attend her unassuming fate.

Stars worship, vastly disappointed
at her queenly dissipate.
Her regal visage, once anointed,
ceases to irradiate.

Stars and moon, assume their turn,
to gallantly now genuflect.
Anticipating sun's return
tomorrow morning, I suspect.

AM I IMPORTANT
April 27, 2015

How important we've become
Myself of course, to me
Just so, is everyone
But when the stuff of life is done
And stone is carved to cover thee
Eternal waiting starts

How important at the time
To me at least, I'll seem
Surprising too, to God divine
For, as earthbound beneath the sod
Devoid of movement, stiff, supine
My spirit graduateth up to God

We've lived this life unto ourselves
And never think that we
Might descend down to earthen shelves
The lie of self importance lies revealed
In lonely graveyard stones
Unvisited in every graveyard field

The wage of sin is everlasting death
Thank God, Christ took my place
While still alive, Christ saveth me
To live for all eternity
'twas nothing ever earned, its free
God's Bible calls it....Grace.

EACH NEW DAY

April 27, 2015

God has a wonderful way
Of lining our days all up in a row
I can't wait for the date
That the calendars show
Is tomorrow morning
But that's every day
And each dreamer doth know
That it's almost brand new
Of course, not almost
I'm just kidding you
We have every assurance
Its never been used
I can't wait to see
What tomorrow has for me
'cause He knows I'll be thankful
And won't be confused
I'll talk to God
That's what folks call prayer
And God will applaud
'cause He's waiting there
To present a new day
My faith in God
I delight to renew
In a prayerful way
How about you

BOB MCCLUSKEY

GOD IN MY KITCHEN
April 26, 2015

Prayer's just God and me in conversation,
or at least, so I've been told.
So when I sit or kneel, or even when I'm walking,
I share with God just how I feel,
my inner heart to God reveal,
but how come I'm the one does all the talking.

I do go on, I know I do, but I have a lot to say,
whilst I hold on to God's rapt attention.
To render my imagination, I see Jesus sitting there,
I set the table up for tea,
a cup for Him, a cup for me,
to help imagine God , I even get another chair.

So there we are, I've set the scene, just God and me,
I'll bet you didn't know He's in my kitchen.
I realize now, the problem in my dire situation
is maybe me, if I'd shut up,
God might speak and even drink another cup,
His cup was dry, or think ye that just might have been......
evaporation?

PROSPERITY'S ILLUSION

April 24, 2015

Thru memory's years
Men have striven for prosperity
Here and there they've had success
To some degree, some more, some less
But always there comes, ultimately
Cruel division of resources
Most walked on foot, a few had horses
Cream they say, will rise to top
But always in the end, you've got
One percent with all the wealth
The rest reducing gradually
To penury or loss of health
There, revolution has its start
Where men rise up against man's greed
That lurks unseen in every heart
Men will die, but most succeed
As was the case in our fair nations
Men fashioning great ships of state
But if you're noticing of late
Alarmingly, with greater speed
The prospering, sad middle class
See all their wealth diminishing
Where has it gone, they cry, alas
Why, gone up to the one percent

And so, fate's wheel is slowly spinning
And will until man's faith doth burn
For Jesus Christ who's Blood will slake
Our need for sin, and will absolve
Man from the death he's in
When man doth strive to give, not take
God's paradise on earth will then begin

HEARTBEAT

April 25, 2015

Tho our feet now cannot
move the way that they used,
and can't even fox trot
in our squeaky old shoes.

Great to see a young couple
Dance with a light heart
Our legs threaten to buckle
e'er we even start.

But if they got a taste
of our rhythm inside,
they'd see youthful slim waist
with a musical glide.

'cause our heart every year
in its squeaky old home,
doth a beat engineer
like a true metronome.

So don't sleep in your seat
when the musicians start,
dance inside to the beat
of your sleepy ole' heart.

BOB MCCLUSKEY

DEATH CAN'T WIN

April 23, 2015

Death, you cannot win!
Forever knocking at our door,
you can't come in.
At least,
you cannot come before
the wages of
destructive sin,
with which you have
evil rapport,
are destined to begin.

Thank God, my sin
didst Jesus know!
And then,
with faithful intercede,
Salvation didst bestow.
God the Father
hung His Son
to take my place
upon the cross, where
once begun,
Christ's precious blood
to cleanse man's sin
forever more doth flow.
Christ's Blood,
Sufficiently doth cleanse
each sinner here below.

TWISTED FINGERS

April 22, 2015

My fingers bending out of shape
to thee, wouldst seemeth wry,
but I keep their bending out of sight,
at least unconsciously, I try.

They accomplish deeds requiring them
to meet my needs, inspiring them
to not decry, but valiantly, to try
in countless ways to tie a bow,
a shoelace or a tie.

The question that did not occur to me
but might to you is, why this plight I'm in?
Since past mid-life I've honored God,
you might think God might thus reward
my strong intent to circumvent all sin.

But sinning in my former life
accomplished every need and every want.
And thus I lingered at the font, of strife
and sowed the seeds you now be witness of,
ergo, these express revelations of God's love.

For sin reaps wages, finally eternal death!
But God allowed this slight unkindness
on each hand, to free me from
gross spiritual blindness,
which in former life didst fashion
sin of such variety, 'twould upset thy propriety,
but Christ yet saved my life, at Gods command.

LEGAL EXECUTION

April 22, 2015

Politicians in our lands
fulfill the law,
the law that plans
to hang the guilty
by the neck
or inject death,
life ends the same.
But who to blame,
the ones who vote,
I guess that's me,
but what the heck,
a death by any name,
please note
is still a death to one
who'll cease to be.

But if we kill
the ones who kill
are we improving
God's superb design?
We do believe
it is God's will
to rescue souls,
consider well the hell
we send them to
beyond the end of time.

BOB MCCLUSKEY

God judges who will die
and judges when,
that's not mans province,
neither you nor I
have mandate to accord
who goes to hell,
tread carefully.
Vengeance is mine,
I will repay
saith the Lord.
Man's vengeance
bodes not well.

WARM ASPHALT

April 21, 2015

A lizard on the asphalt lay,
luxuriating in the heat
remaining from a sunny day,
transferring through his feet.
That activating temperature
if he would move,
he knew for sure
he had to keep.

The darkness
coming over him
is friendly, he can hide.
But bright lights
running over him,
charging from the night,
warn, it is no longer safe
to linger longer in this place.
That roaring beast
would soon efface
the pattern from his hide.

Quite startling, his alacrity
evading thus, that beast
who tried to place a tire tread
upon his back
from tail to head, at least.

From side of road
he watched as night,
swallowed beasty
out of sight of his abode.
Then just to demonstrate delight,
he ate a toad.

OFFSHORE ACCENT

April 20, 2015

I spoke on the phone today,
to my computer provider.
This required I relate
to computer from "start",
in my ninety year state
I responded quite late,
this might even be
hard on my heart.
Back and forth didst relay,
from one hand on my mouse
in the other hand, phone
to delight of my spouse
who happened to be home today.
I interrupted her pleasure to say,
I'm now very confused,
Feeling very ill used,
'twould be nice if you'd just go away.
I next spoke in the phone
to a lady from Rome, or
some country located offshore.
With her accent intense
I required she repeat,
What she said made no sense,
my remarkable feat
was to last to the end,
and maintain my aplomb,
I aint call'n that number no more.

BOB McCLUSKEY

But it made me feel kinda neat,
'cause that lady from Rome
on the end of my phone,
spoke with words incomplete,
I think it was Greek.

IF I REALLY COULD FLY

April 23, 2015

If I really could fly, would it matter?
I mean matter to me, it's easy to see
that it matters to birds,
tho they likely don't know
just, away they go
on a plane that is groovy, not flatter.
For they swoop and they dive
just to stay alive,
to feed, they speed
and meet every need, aloft on the wing
as they flutter and sing, they chatter.

So, the question is, could I make it my biz
to eat while my feet, just suspend?
Whilst controlling my wings
could I manage those things,
not fall from the sky
whilst I really do fly, not pretend.
I think God was right
when He cancelled our flight
whilst here on the earth,
but I'll have my new birth
then for all that I'm worth,
boy will I ever fly
in the great by and by.

ETERNAL HOPE

April 19, 2015

Whence comes the emptiness
that lurketh in man's heart.
That nameless, cold unrecognized
desire which, even though despised
will not depart.

With wants and needs all being met,
he's still unsatisfied.
Those grown up toys which he deploys
do thrill at first, but soon these joys
be tainted with regret.

Man looks for hope, in all the things
he doth consume.
But fulfillment just seems more remote,
life becomes more difficult to cope,
to hope resume.

Outside of God, there is no way to cope!
If life's burdens lay a heavy toll,
God tells the pathway to your goal.
Give wealth away to bless the poor,
then follow Christ, the way to your
eternal hope.

GOD OR GAIN

April 18, 2015

Were any acts of kindness
on our part, translated into gold,
would we be rich?
Didst we betimes,
a heavy heart make bold
by our encouragement.
If converted to
pecuniary measurement,
which I agree,
wouldst treasure me.
Would I then
with noble motive spent,
remain content.

We cannot serve two masters,
God once said,
we'll love the one,
the other we will hate.

This indicates
that I must therefore make
a choice twixt God
and common gain,
the one be blessed,
the other renders pain
with attributes
to rearrange my mien
from cleanliness
to attributes unclean.
The choice for me
remaineth clear and plain,
without a doubt
I choose God over gain.

WOMAN'S LOVELINESS

April 17, 2015

To woman in her Godly loveliness, I sing!
Unconsciously she launches dreams,
a lovely careless thing she seems.
Yet somehow knowingly doth bring
a world that's filled with everything
desirable.

A woman young, of course has just begun
to broadcast all her loveliness abroad.
To raise within the hearts of men
a hunger, for the moment when
they might progress to be the one
to win her love, to then become
the Romeo all other men, applaud.

But also to all slightly older women, who
unconsciously, or maybe not so much,
have also added that enthralling touch
of Godly grace that draws men to pursue.
To simply just be near enough, to taste
the unintended wafting sweet bouquet
flowing in their wake, that doth all men undo.
To mature woman, in her Godly loveliness,
I also sing.

PEPPERMENT STICK
April 16, 2015

Ya gotta be quick
If ya gets a stick
Of peppermint candy
That's nice and thick
The first guy ya sees
Will ask for a lick
That's why I said
Ya gotta be quick
He'll ask for a lick
But he'll take a bite
Before ya knows it
You're in a fight
It happened to me
Just the other night
I hurt my knuckles
On his hard head
Today Mom told me
To stay in bed
So I takes off for bed
Like a smokin' rocket
And smuggles me candy
Outa me pocket
If I eats it all
I'm gonna be sick
But that's what a guy does
With a peppermint stick

THE WAR WAS LONG

April 15, 2015

The war was long, I knew that I
Could not forevermore defy
The odds
We were engaged, we did attack
The ones enraged were shooting back
It didn't hurt, I heard the smack
I found that laying on my back
As silence reigned, delivered peace
No sound remained, I felt release
I felt the wetness at my waist
Gazing straight up at the sky
I marveled at the clouds that I
Could view in solitude
This must be how it feels to die
Somehow, I didn't like the taste
Of life's remaining interlude
This cannot be, no, no, not me
I'm far too healthy, far too young
My song of life was hardly sung
Do I hear voices, ours or theirs
Hold on kid, Fred, staunch that wound
Gently now, I think he swooned
Help me lift him on the board
Together now, all one accord
He's gonna make it, I can tell
He's lasted thru this very well

BOB MCCLUSKEY

God sent me help, it had to be
Now Mom can go to church with me
That guy was right, I'm here to tell
When he opined that..."war is hell"

OF COURSE I CARE

April 14, 2015

Of the current assault against Christians
all over the world, I've become aware.
Do I care, of course I care!
Every Christian in our fair land
would quickly reply the same,
as would Christians everywhere.
But how does God know that I care,
or that anyone else is even aware
of this shame.
Well, our recourse is to pray,
for it seems the only way
we have to save these brothers.
But a deadly silence is all I hear
from the Church, initiating fear
as my faith, this outrage smothers.

But, what am I saying,
don't I believe that the prayer we share
is enough to relieve the horror they're going thru.
Is God not big enough to bring
us grandly to victory thru this thing,
this repulsive manifestation of hate,
is our prayer too small, does it come too late,
but why am I asking you?

I need to face this question myself,
tho even as I ask, I know
that God works all things together for good,
and I must face up to this truth as I should,
thru persecution God's Church doth grow.
The effectual fervent prayer
of a righteous man availeth much, I know.
Thus, for the sake of those persecuted so,
I'd better get fervent, and stay in touch with God
for my faith to grow.

SATAN'S YOKE

April 13, 2015

For some, discernment has to wait
perhaps, till latter years.
Till man doth totter, t'wards the gate
behind which lieth each man's fate,
for many, each man's fears.

Admitted, there be Born Again ones,
whether old or young.
Man mostly bows to life's deceptions,
when God displays these sweet exceptions,
exultant songs be sung.

The rest of us plod on thru life,
forever looking down.
See nothing out beyond our nose,
to where God's lovely garden grows,
beyond the edge of town.

Where born again folk, ever frolic
midst Gods vested joys.
Where God sets people alcoholic
free, to romp in these symbolic
vales so peaceful, so bucolic,
God deploys.

BOB MCCLUSKEY

So, if you'd like to join these folk,
in God's unmerited favor.
Receive Jesus as God spoke,
divest thyself of Satan's yoke,
God's blessings you will savor.

GOD SENDS OTHER SAVIORS

April 16, 2015

The saviors of mankind come from amongst men,
Oh, I don't mean man's ultimate Savior.
He is God, and of course comes from heaven when
we least expect to be apprehended.
By then its too late, our revolt is ended
by love.

But the saviors to whom I refer, in a sense
Simply do not exist, we can't see them.
They would manifest love, oft without recompense,
if all appears lost, and we're grounded in fear.
Without counting the cost, these saviors appear
from above.

When I say from above, from above they're directed
by God, to save men from impending disaster.
Unannounced, their arrival is never expected,
might be a back bench politician, elected
who's valor lay hid for this time, undetected,
for when push comes to shove.

At least that's how God moved in our turbulent past,
but God forever might not strive with man.
The times be a-changin' and changin' fast,
as we venture the days God refers to as "last".
Seek Salvation my friend, just as fast as you can,
in Jesus' love.

BOB MCCLUSKEY

LOVE'S ENOUGH

April 12, 2015

The hours of life
flow silent past,
life's clock
doth no one see.
We know not,
whether slow or fast
life's falter comes,
but God's love lasts,
and that's enough for me.

We strive thru life's
unfolding years,
whate'er our status be.
Life brings its share
of scalding tears,
but God's love quiets
all my fears,
and that's enough for me.

Behold, as rows
of lettered stones,
in silence, beckon me.
They hunger
to devour my bones,
but in my heart,
God's love intones,
and that's enough for me.

THIS WORLD

April 11, 2015

God spoke it
Man broke it
Within a
Short time
From the time
Man awoke, it
Was murder
And mayhem
With Satan
To stoke it
With deceit
In man's heart
From the start
To evoke it
Yet God in His word
Tho absurd
Didst denote it
Would yet
Bring us thru
At the end
Me and you
To forgiveness
From Jesus
Whose blood
Ever frees us

BOB MCCLUSKEY

From death
In His place
Even tho
We rebelled
With blood guilt
On our face
Which man
Could not erase
To release us

WHAT FORCE

April 10, 2015

What is that force
Within us all
That gets us out of bed
At dawn
And help us with
Our underwear
Before of course
With savoir fare
We pulls our pants
And sneakers on
And then by growling
Hunger led
We eats our porridge
With a spoon
Anticipating we'd be fed
Another bowl of mush
At noon
It cannot be
I don't believe it
What decides
I must relieve it
Only to make room
For more
What's happening
Inside of me
What force provides
The destiny

Of stuff inside
My stomach storage
If that's the way
It has to be
I hope that I
Will never see
Another bowl
Of transient porridge

GOD SIMPLY SPOKE

April 10, 2015

Is God real?
Of course God's real,
everyone knows it.
Or at least, God knows it,
and maybe a handful
of others who feel,
that perhaps it's wrong
to murder and steal,
thus, would not oppose it.
Also, how did you learn
to discern, not deny,
God is able to hang
all those stars In the sky.
Using nothing it seems
like a scaffold or rope,
not e'er in his dreams
could man ever cope.
And the wonderment is
God exercised His
prerogative
to create everything
God simply spoke.
To make man alive
God blew into his nose.

BOB MCCLUSKEY

So forget evolution
And all that jive,
God designed fingers
to give a high five,
not a high four
like I told you before.

DO WE KNOW GOD

April 11, 2015

Do we really know God
Oh, we say we do
And I count myself
Amongst those who review
Every circumstance
With a mind to eschew
The lie that Jesus
Cannot be true
For I know that God
Will sometimes split
The veil twixt us
A little bit
I speak as one
With first person account
So its chiselled in stone
And there's no amount
Of intellectual dispute
That can deter me
From the wonderful truth
I now plainly see
That God loveth me
But its equally true
God loves all men
Need I remind
That this includes
even little ole' you
All eternity thru

BOB MCCLUSKEY

AVANT-GARDE ARE
APOSTATE

April 7, 2015

So much in this world remains static,
whilst at the same time, the times change.
They adversely become quite erratic,
metamorphosized, they rearrange.

Just take painting, a subject at hand,
now evolved into rabid debate.
Classic art depicts life, as quite grand,
the avant-garde have become apostate.

Will old masters somehow, reappear,
bringing sanity back to the fold.
The art-wheel still revolves, never fear,
masters new might evolve from the old.

Much the same, women's fashion in clothes,
designed by odd fellows gone mad.
Goodness knows their ensembles look strange,
if they don't soon return to the styles they once had,
I'm head'n back home on the range.

NO SENSE OF ART

April 6, 2015

How can such simple presentations,
designed to play a part.
Defy art's usual designations,
rectangled, artless imitations,
present themselves as art.

Often simply colors, paneled,
displaying hues alternately.
Water colored or enameled,
with a sense of art, untrammeled,
sure beats me.

Would be art aficionados,
view with head at measured slant.
Uttering their ah's and oh's,
what do they see, would you suppose,
that us poor peasants can't.

I'll share with you, a revelation,
if you promise not to tell.
Art critics would not make a fuss
If they surveyed like one of us,
they just can't see that well.

BOB MCCLUSKEY

POTENTIAL POETS

April 6, 2015

Potential poets, at the start,
write from intensity of heart.
Whilst others, sensing smell of honey,
undertake to write for money.
Realities cruel choice confliction
drives some then to writing fiction,
swearing nevermore to rhyme.
They turn to prose with great elation,
but sensing hunger's invitation
from their stomachs all the time,
they take some job below their station,
sacrificing life's creation.
But after work, their avocation
creates poetry sublime.

FOOLISH LAD

April 4, 2015

A foolish lad of doubtful mien,
wouldst tilt at windmills it doth seem.
It made him glad when shadow seen,
as on his paper lance he'd lean.

I saw him, at his shadow glance,
as shadow mimicked every prance
he took, with his evasive dance
to outmaneuver shadow,
and to thus romance bravado,
it would seem.

But silliness at last won out,
for when the sun didst start to wane,
our foolish lad began to shout
at shadow's unexpected rout,
to loud acclaim.

He thrust his paper lance at it,
as fading shadow's proud disdain
deflected it.
With loud proclaim, our silly twit
objected it.

BOB McCLUSKEY

Referring to the rough terrain,
He charged that shadow
just to win the game, selected it.
So by default, he gave himself the victory,
as sun was waning once again,
ejected it.

WILD ROSE GARDEN

April 2, 2015

There existeth in a place to which I ventured,
a large garden seeming wild and lacking care.
With unresponsive blossoms being censured,
I found so many roses dying there.

Roses rooted well and starting boldly,
thrusting upward with impressive length.
But seemingly, all care rejected coldly,
exulting it would seem, in their own strength.

The Gardener who would come, suffered rejecting,
he wept, for well he knew what lay ahead.
If they submit not to his pruning and inspecting,
to his careful apprehending and selecting,
each healthy, growing rose would soon be dead.

So, stretching from afar with love extended,
He yet offered guarantee to tend them well.
He reached them where they were, those who contended,
And some didst pay attention, I could tell.

When harvest time arrived, some seemed to be
responsive to his love, who then were qualified
to grace the Gardener's house as progeny,
whilst others gnashed their teeth before they died.

They knew somehow, the blessing they rejected,
grieving oh so very much, the choice life gives.
Each rose must e'er be pruned to be perfected,
be free from spot or blemish when inspected,
this must of course occur, whilst each rose lives.

THE STATUS QUO

April 2, 2015

With the status quo, our nation is found
satisfied, near the top of the heap.
In relative terms of course, I expound,
for the rest of the world is gaining ground,
right now, even as we speak.

This would be ok, if along the way
as they rose, we did not fall back.
But I'm sorry to say,
if greed gets in the way,
we could suffer a famine attack.

If our attitude smacks of complacency,
if we ever neglect to pray.
It would only take, one lost harvest to break
the staff of life, with no flour to bake
our bread, what a desperate day.

We could always buy from the other guy,
grain from his bountiful yield.
But if rain never came for them as well,
they would not be able to trade or sell,
grain to us from an empty field.

So if food would grow, on our knees we must go
to God with heartfelt intercession.
To repent of sin, invite Jesus in,
lay the groundwork for mercy, that God would begin
to deliver our land from oppression.

SOME HEAR ANGELS SING

April 3, 2015

Some navigate life
with a smile and a song,
they seem to hear angels inside.
We love to be with them,
to travel along
in their wake, or to walk alongside.

Whilst others don't seem
to fit life very well,
as they carry a scowl or a sneer.
We try to avoid them
I'm sorry to tell,
whatever inside must they hear.

I'm sure they're not hearing God's angels sing,
this is evident from their facade.
If tuned into bedlam from hell, I know,
they'd hear demented screams
from men burning below,
as they cry out for mercy from God.

BOB McCLUSKEY

PASSING LOVE'S TEST

April Fool's Day, 2015

Love is a delicate blossoming flower,
delighting in admiration.
Love will not entertain an utterance sour,
'twill drain all affection upon the hour,
and cause untold consternation.

For love is so easily damaged and bruised,
when unkindness be manifest.
Sweet lover respondeth by feeling ill used,
by a love correspondent who standeth accused,
of failing to pass love's test.

So, when guilty of thoughtless, disastrous exchange,
This insensitive lout must retreat.
Then convenient tryst, subsequently arrange,
at a place she would never assess as strange,
and throw his miserable hulk at her feet.

IS WINTER OVER

March 31, 2015

God waketh up
one clarion seed
from the icy grip
of winter's wheeze,
to sleepily slip
by slow degrees
into wakefulness,
his God to please.
But, get a grip,
how do all seeds know
at the very same time,
that it's time to grow.
I know! I know!
I listened below,
and heard the first
to awake cry out,
Wake up! Wake up!
I heard him shout.
All the other seeds
with a toss of head,
with shudder and shake
got out of bed.
The first one shouted
When I count three,
c'mon you guys
just follow me.

And all at once
thru the earth
they burst,
in unison
all followed the first.
So, mystery solved,
that's how seeds know
when its time to grow.

TRUSTY DANDY-LION
March 31, 2015

If I had to be a lovely flower,
I know the one I'd like to be.
I'd like to be a Dandy-Lion,
make everyone afraid of me.

Then, as a trusty Dandy-Lion,
I could make a fearful roar.
But, frum all my lusty tryin,
my throat is feelin awful sore.

Just when I was feelin fearful,
a Butterfly lit right on me.
I'd love to give him quite an earful,
if I could roar, I'd make him flee.

My landlord is the local lawn grower,
each year he amputateth me.
My roar would make him flee his lawn mower,
or cut a circle right round me.

With one big roar, I'd start him shakin,
then when he comes, I'd duck down low.
But without my roar, my head's forsaken,
for another year, I'll have to go.

GOD, COME LIE WITH ME

March 30, 2015

God, come lie with me on the limp, warm grass,
in a world washed free of the cruel and crass,
where just for a while, I'll be free at last
in God's ecstasy.

In God's ecstasy of creation displayed,
I'll hide from the worries of life's parade,
whilst admiring exquisite perfection arrayed,
for pure hearts to see.

I'll look at the structure of one small ant,
at the faultless design that God didst grant,
to enable his travel from plant to plant,
so worry free.

With my head on the earth in reclining pose,
I'll admire the desire of each budding rose,
to blossom where God's perfect garden grows,
in the heart of me.

And when at last, from the evening's chill
I arise, and devise a fire that will
add warmth to God's loving embrace, until
He is part of me.

HE MUST INCREASE IN ME

March 29...2015

Despite our sin, God so loved the world
in the state we were in,
He gave His only begotten Son
that whosoever believeth in Him
in this world so filled with strife,
should not perish but might evermore begin,
an everlasting life.

For God sent not His Son into the world
to condemn the world,
but that the world through Him might be saved.
The whole world be saved, not only a few,
because Jesus Christ the omniscient, knew
the whole world was lost and depraved.

But then, after we're saved...I say after,
for before, we could not ever know
the reason we must be sanctified,
we could never begin to grow,
in the knowledge of God, as hard as we try,
God's Spirit must open each blinded eye.

BOB MCCLUSKEY

When John said Christ must increase, meant he,
out and about in the world.
Oh no, I now see what John really meant,
I now understand, his specific intent
was that Jesus must increase, in you and me
to the glory that God the Father would see.

DOWN STAIR

March 28, 2015

As I lounge in my boudoir
down stair,
Whilst life's antic
be frantic above.
Higher up in the sky
somewhere,
God determinates why
He should favor this guy,
yet He blesses
my labor with love.

So I try
to anonymous be,
in endeavor
to make little noise.
In this place where I live
as my landlord doth give
great acceptance to me
whilst exemplarily,
I bleed poetry
with enviable poise.

ALL STRIVING ENDS
March 28, 2015

All striving ends!
One must obey that call
from God to everyone,
not audible, yet unassailable
to strangers or to friends.
None can be unavailable,
no one contends.

All striving ends!
As end it must, obeying then the law
Of God's well planned obsolesce,
When all the parts that distant day
At life's begin, were light and gay.
Gone, bygone years of adolesce,
life's dividends.

All striving ends!
Of sore regrets I have a few,
things I should have featured then
to help life come out differently.
I should have come to Jesus when
my days were young, I did eschew
a life with Christ, I never knew
how blessed, fulfilled, when life doth be
as God intends.

LUCK

May 28, 2015

Luck is a nonentity
Luck does not exist
Outcomes occur
When your way you insist
They end well or they don't
You never can tell
But you can't blame luck
If they don't end well
Good or bad luck
Has nothing to do
At the end of the day
With what happens to you
It just depends
On chances one takes
On how one contends
On decisions one makes
So don't blame luck
When down you lay
And tuck yourself in
But forget to pray
Luck does not enter
Your situation
You are the cause
Of your own aggravation

God will direct
Your life if you try
To trust in Jesus
Before you die

GOD OFFERS ABSOLUTION
March 27, 2015

Who amongst us would insist,
when struck upon the cheek
resoundly, with an open fist,
to offer up the other cheek
with manner trite, submissive, meek,
doth such a one exist.

Or when confronted in a spate
of anger and confusions.
Doth yet exist a saintly saint
to ever offer love for hate,
fighting off the need to faint
whilst bandaging contusions.

But rather, rife amongst the folk
with whom I oft do congregate.
Are those who freely spread the cloak
of normal inhumanity.
They would not e'er necessitate
this lapse into insanity.

But do not submit to utter gloom,
God proffers us, solution.
He promised, He's returning soon
to give us strength to play our part,
receiving Christ into our heart
for precious absolution.

BOB MCCLUSKEY

LIFE'S DREADED FEAR

March 27, 2015

Ah life!
How sweetly doth it run its course,
although without direction it would seem.
Thru wedded bliss or lurking, cruel divorce,
becoming in the end, a waking dream.

What purpose, only to exist alive,
such purpose seemeth wasted here.
To what end doth man blindly strive,
what insurance, against what deadly fear.

Such insurance cannot profit, at the end,
thou vainly raiseth up a false defense.
Against what dreaded fate doth thou contend,
false hope can't circumvent thy journey hence.

May I with much kindness, now present
insurance, which cometh with a guarantee.
Ensuring thy eternal, sweet content,
'twill not expire for all eternity.

A guarantee from life's creator grand,
Lord Jesus Christ, whose word cannot be nullified.
Fear not, reach up, take Christ's extended hand
from Calvary's Cross, you are the reason Jesus died.

TOO LATE! TOO LATE!

June 14, 2011

Lord, Oh Lord, your warnings come
at inconvenient time.
Too soon to think of heaven, Lord,
my freedom you'd confine.

There's yet a lot of life to live,
a lot of girls to court;
a lot of food, a lot of drink,
and babies to abort.

A lot of sin to yet enjoy,
to lust and fornicate;
a lot of gossiping to do,
and lies to fabricate.

Then when I'm old and had my fun,
I'll happily arrange,
to say the prayer that gets me there,
I've time to make that change.

What's this, what's this; you say I'm dead,
the fate that I did fear.
This isn't right, it isn't fair,
No warning did I hear.

What sombre voice accosts me now,
attesting to this truth.
God's clarion trumpet warning me,
Christ's gospel from my youth.

Too late, too late, Oh God, too late,
there is no going back.
Life's race is run, the die is cast,
as picture fades to black.

CHILDREN AT PLAY

March 26, 2015

Children at play; we see them as they shake
out a pecking order, yet unconsciously
responding to either fear or indignation
whilst endeavoring to make
a way at play, to satisfy each little need.
They either fearlessly repulse
an intimidating toy stealer
whilst tearlessly, no matter girl or boy
they indignantly repel an interruption
to their own innate greed.
Or fearfully, they tearfully give in
to an invaders intimidating ploy,
and timidly relinquishing their little toy
they acquiesce with fearful speed.
Meanwhile, each exchange is a revelation
of life's projected interchange of feelings,
with other peoples indignations
manifesting life's frustrations,
will we afford them understanding
of future life's demanding,
will we teach them all they need.

GRANT ME IMPUNITY

March 24, 2015

We offhandedly say, "how Ya Dooin"
When we really just mean "Hello"
This can lead us to rack and rooin
With someone we hardly know
We might look at the sky
And resoundly decry
The spate, of late
Of waters that try
To circumvent our umbrella
Whilst we wonder why
We even try
When we hardly know the fella
When at last he flees
We can hear him say
In a silent voice
As he walks away
"Lord, I ask you please"
I still hear him pray
With ardent importunity
"grant me the grace
If I again see his face
To disappear with impunity"

LOVELY PINK SPEEDO

March 23, 2015

I endeavor to weather perfection
But always pursue wrong direction
Moral compass, it seems
Came apart at the seams
As I gobbled up every confection

So I made a new start yesterday
To overcome indolent weakness
Threw my chocolate away
Now I'm sorry to say
That pies fulfill my completeness

So I overturned now a new leaf
My endeavor I tempered like steel
I just close my eyes
When I pass chocolate pies
But much pain in my stomach I feel

So away with this great sacrificing
All this starving has killed my libido
I just swallowed my pride
And now flaunt my backside
At the beach in my lovely pink speedo

BOB MCCLUSKEY

OUR NATION AS A HOUSE

March 22, 2015

Our nation as a house doth stand
in satisfied complacence.
Our roof protecteth out of hand,
our reputation standeth grand,
whilst Inuit schools across the land
indulge in gross decadence.

Destruction we have kept at bay,
we've strengthened sin's defences.
Greed hidden from the light of day,
too big to fail banks, don't repay,
whilst fleshly lusts, indulge away
our over active senses.

But nations will, as well as men
come under judgement, consequently
one important fact will tell
God of their judgement evidently,
when He rewards their treatment
of His nation, Israel.

Blood spilleth all across God's earth,
dead prematurely see,
God's view of all their sin since birth,
their conduct, God will reimburse,
by blessing or eternal curse
to them, to you, to me.

AWAY WITH RAIN

March 21, 2015

Away with thee, thou wet and cold,
thin rain that falls on door and sash.
My battered window panes of old,
were threatened by sin's thunder crash.

My roof be sound, my walls be stout,
they guard in grand resist to thee.
Thy prying threat cavorts without,
but shall not sprinkle sin on me.

My castle walls be girded well
with Godly trough and gutter pipe.
They deflect all thy waves that fell
upon my roof throughout the night.

So redirect thy tiresome drenching
from God's garden, standing by.
Thou cannot breach our strong entrenching,
Though our verdure gaspeth dry.

Godly rain, we now shall laud,
for bringing verdure into greening.
All thirsty men shall now applaud
God's sweet deluge, man's faith redeeming.

SO HE DIED
April 18, 2015

Everybody is going to die!
Every last one, be assured!
I know a friend
who said he demurred,
with a cognitive factor
undoubtedly blurred.
When his demise occurred
I tried,
as hard as I could
to tell him he lied.
For the bed
he now occupied,
was a place for the dead,
so the source of his dread
snuck up upon Ned
and could not be denied,
so he died!

SATAN'S LIES INSANE, ABSURD

March 21, 2015

May I not be a one to care
for inconsequential oddities.
For detriments which linger there,
vain would be prodigies.

One to respond to Satan's prods
from hell fire's glow.
To worship other would be gods
from down below.

Much more wouldst I, with vision clear
hold truths, resplendent in God's Word.
Where lieth principles held dear,
not Satan's lies inane, absurd.

When cometh then, that fateful day
of judgement, may I e'er be one
who heareth well his Savior say
so sweetly to his ear, "Well Done".

BOB MCCLUSKEY

If thy heart also, well refrains
from Satan's dull despondencies,
thou wouldst then, have thy spirit free.
If man whilst earthbound, Christ receives,
God's grand forgive from sin reprieves,
he'll be with God throughout eternity.

MOTHER TREE

March 20, 2015

Beloved one, thru passing years,
and years that yet do onward flow.
You tenderly enhanced the flowers
that graced your earthly garden's show.
With love, when barely more than seed
you fed and watered each new sprout.
You mothered every plaintive need
whilst keeping all destruction out.
You lovingly matured each charge,
not one didst e'er succumb to blight.
From babies, they've now grown quite large,
what e'er you did, you did it right.
So now, these flower have ever gone
to different gardens of their choosing.
But nuts fall not far from mother tree,
to flourish there for God to see,
not one fell, to their losing.

SO MANY HILLS
March 17, 2015

So many hills surround us, yet without
significance, it seems.
In romantic times, hills might become
a trysting place, to meet with one
whose heart consumes our waking dreams,
it ever seems.

Yet other seven hills lie prone
where grandeur flaunteth plain.
That ancient place man calleth Rome
provideth Vatican, a home,
whilst thru the years, quite famous
it became.

One hill remaineth, to yet legislate
men's soul's eternal designation.
To arbitrate twixt love and hate,
thru love, men's souls repatriate,
Golgotha filleth every nation
with Salvation.

WHAT OF THE MIND

March 16, 2015

What of the mind!
With age, we all become a little smaller,
doth the intellect in every man
that's designated mind, conversely grow yet taller,
even kind!

Or as we grow old!
Doth the aging mind digress from hospitality,
dispensing with, in discontent all sweet conviviality.
This is a lurking danger to our mental re-arranger,
we've been told!

Or humorless!
This too is a lurking danger, at least in part I guess,
because of pain's afflictions, we so stoically support.
Whilst our secret parts, with one another can't cavort
in manner entertaining, because of all the paining
we suppress!

So send it back to hell!
Its the product of the Devil, all of Satan's integrating
pain in bone and muscle, doth prevent our undertaking
things we once did very well, so return it to the pit
where devils dwell, Amen,
Yea, return it to the pit where devils dwell!

BOB MCCLUSKEY

DISEMBODIED

March 14, 2015

What, in a poet's scratching
doth attract me
thus attaching, this reader
to a writer, who appears
to hide his face.

Tis then,
not that poet lieth,
its in fact the poet's books.
Full of poems, that he plieth
whilst he's covering his looks.

He so boldly is appearing
in his disembodied thrall.
His pen then, superseding
a portrayal of his bleeding,
as he suffereth poet's call.

With embryonic dealing
he's the vendor of lines writ.
His intense poetic feeling
for God's poetry, revealing
lyric splendor, no pretender
after all.

DESIRES DECLINING YEARS

March 14, 2015

I was born to be a man
with needs, but more than needs,
with wants beyond the needs,
that all athirst require or ever can admire,
and for which unrequited lusting
ever bleeds.

And lusts for what, for that which never,
after vile consumption, satisfies.
For when in time the sated lust doth rise again,
its satisfaction unfulfilled, converts to pain
for all the ecstasy, when satiation dies,
cannot remain.

How merciful, that God designed the pall
which falls upon desire's declining years.
Negating now, those raging appetites
and yet somehow, projects a weakened call,
surviving from somewhere between the ears,
or not at all.

I called man's elderly condition, merciful,
for now, the thoughts of his eternity
will hopefully, not be distracted
by those desires and wants enacted
in man's mind, so common to us all.
To heed God's invitation, so protracted
thru the centuries, Salvation's call.

SANDS OF TIME

March 13, 2015

Behold, it seemeth only
one short hour ago,
our hourglass sand
lay almost all above
the empty bottom half,
awaiting there, our life
to exercise prerogatives.
But now observe,
much sands
be trickling down below
where history lives
accumulating there,
fast doth it grow.
One hopes, perhaps
a clump of sand
wouldst fatefully
restrict the flow,
impeding then,
perhaps in part
the emptying.

But secretly, we know
God keeps our heart;
God's finger holds
life's buttons,
and whilst our sand
remaineth stubbornly
above the flow,
God holds our button
clearly designated,
GO!
But, when all life's sands
have emptied from the top,
God will depress our button
clearly designated,
STOP!

A BABY MYSTERY

March 12, 2015

I gazed upon a mystery
One day in baby's cot
The little one
Seemed vacillating
Staring upward
Looking not
At me
I wondered,
In his little mind
What did the baby
Seem to find
So captivatingly
A vacant smile
Crept o'er his face
But nothin else
Seemed out of place
It then occurred to me
The little rascal
Found release
Which filled him
With that look of peace
He was enjoying
A delightful pee.

LA PAZ BOLIVIA

March 12, 2015

Oh to write a little poem
Startling in its genius
I called, but you weren't home
You were always one to roam
It never should have been thus
I was come to tell you that
I could no longer see you
Your key was underneath the mat
You were gone, where were you at
My words could not now free you
You would still regard me as
Your covert possession
I was done with all that jazz
That was my confession
I was off to see La Paz
Freed from all thy trivia
Here is your house key that I took
If you should ever care to look
That city's in Bolivia
Farewell

REBELLIOUSNESS
March 12, 2015

Oh God of clear unbridled recitation,
come to those deprived, despaired of hope.
To those who suffer in their deprivation,
separate from the Word's vast stimulation,
enable them insight, to ever cope.

Renew them, in their bare, unguarded prisons,
barless prisons of the mind, where hope is lost.
Repay them not in kind, but give them visions,
requiring of them, spiritual decisions,
for which Jesus on that day, didst pay the cost.

These lost yet ever would be rank digressers
o'er sheepfold walls, avoiding Godly doors.
Unknowing, they've become inept possessors
of inanities, of which they are confessors,
midst the freedoms their rebelliousness ignores.

So Lord, we give them over to your kindness,
and pray the scales from off their blinded eyes.
When light of truth at last they see,
the name of Jesus Christ will be
a benediction, cursing they'll despise.

GARDEN DESECRATION
March 12, 2015

We come again, to that sweet wine
of life's resurgence which, in time
doth follow after Valentine,
I speak of blessed spring.

Ah spring, how welcome, thy resurgence
from pale winter's abdication.
Green grass carpets re-emergence
of life's deadly speculation.

How gently doth God's warming beam
caress each smiling, upturned face.
Softly, spring's sweet zephyrs seem,
the cares of winter, to erase.

Then, as the month progresses slowly,
Satan's truculence succeeds
in our garden's desecration, with unholy,
cursed weeds....Ah Spring.

LAST DISASTER

March 12, 2015

Fare thee well
my pretty friends,
as life's grand way
among thee wends.
For a season
thou and I
fashioned thru
keen ear or eye
repartee
to reason by.
To give and take
our thirst to slake
for information
then to make
conclusion by.
But all be hollow
all be dust
in time et al
must follow after.
Burn or rust
slower or faster,
paths of glory
cannot save
that final journey
to the grave,
man's last disaster.

OUR LOVE
March 11, 2015

Ah Love, so sweetly,
yet so fecklessly bestows,
in reckless apprehension
of the hour
when lovelight glows,
her ancient intervention,
none aware of God's intention
apropos.

Sweet love's ephemerality!
So delicately doth heart meet
one haunting visage,
trance like in her beauty,
intoxicating, sweet.
Love then invades
this naive heart's repose.

And so love goes,
ever old, yet ever new!
With God's invention
penetrating me and you,
to seal the fate
of our poor hearts
the Holy Spirit slew.
Jesus ever enervating
our resplendent love,
so sweet, so new.

BEAUTY FOR ASHES

March 11, 2015

Ugliness vies with beauty,
with flags unfurled
relentlessly, for all to see,
across God's world.
Where, rampant
in its ugly strength,
man's hidden,
vile propensity
for ugliness, at length
doth seem to overcome
each attribute of beauty,
with destruction
as man's duty
in each battle won.

But beauties virtuous deploy
lies oft unseen, to faithfully
true hearts then buoy,
despite all effort to destroy
man's virtuous dream.
Sin subsequently doth array
in depth of human hearts.
But God didst promise.....

BOB MCCLUSKEY

"Beauty for ashes,
the oil of joy for mourning,
the garment of praise
for the spirit of heaviness;
that they might be called
trees of righteousness,
the planting of the Lord,
that He might be glorified."
Amen.

EACH LEAF RENEWED

March 11, 2015

A tree becomes the world
to every leaf, resplendent there.
At first as buds, in symphony uncurled,
to breathe a benediction on the air.

So fragile, every leaf designed to see
a union, with a promised Prince of Peace.
Their transpiration circulates to free
this promise, giving every leaf release.

Perhaps its leafy foliage doth conceal
a secret place where life is tucked away.
Where moth cannot corrupt, nor any steal,
where leaves await a promised judgement day.

Each tree's indestructible iron trunk,
doth seem to be impervious to wear.
But just as trees fall to the earth,
this world, despite enormous girth
will be renewed God promises, one day,
one day when leaves no longer die away.

LIFE'S HARVEST
March 10, 2015

What then, leave we when we go?
Is our little field well watered,
all ill's harbingers well slaughtered,
as to end of life we tottered,
weed we well each nascent row.

Our field of life was delegated
by the Lord, I'll have you know.
God determined when He sent you
to observe each weed event, you
wouldst endeavor when He lent you
Living Words, to then prevent you
from destruction as you go.

So, as we approach the day of reckon,
better tidy up our field.
We won't hear God's Reaper beckon
as he tally's up life's yield.
While there's time, let's get to hoeing
for we have no way of knowing
what He'll harvest from our sowing,
eternal destiny be sealed.

IT'S ABOUT TIME

March 9, 2015

How brief, the time allotted when
at life's begin, we helpless come
unknowing, to the challenges that lie
through briefest years for every man
ere time doth fly.

How careless, how so profligate our waste
of precious time, metered into fleeting hours
by man's design, according to his taste.
Man's clocks record the hours as they pass,
unconscious of how weeks and months
recede into lost nothingness, alas.

What of friends, who's lives we came to know,
as time transpired they disappeared,
where, in or out of time I wonder, did they go.
Were they as profligate with time as I
to leave this sphere, or are they here,
yet unaware as I, of time's vast flow.

There is a place where time doth not exist,
where, at each man's end of time we all must go.
To blessing or to cursing doth depend
I have discovered, on choices we insist
we have the right to make, although.
The place we choose by godly obedience or defiance,
placing all our trust in science, or deciding our reliance
on Lord Jesus, is up on high to ever be with God,
or thru eternity's forever, isolated down below.
But God doth know.

JUDGING

March 7, 2014

So thoughtlessly
we venture in,
to judge another's part.
Only outward stuff we see
God sees man's inner heart.
God sternly tells us
not to do it,
therefore we should
get right to it,
from sin depart.

And since we know
it is a sin to
judge, to God deride.
We never should begin to,
know ye
God doth currently
look into
our remarks
strangely akin to
Satan's pride.

Therefore, we should
be forsooking, judging
with great danger fraught.
Wherefore,
since God might be looking,
chance is good,
our goose be cooking,
surely we shalt
in our sin,
be sorely caught.

EVERY LIVING THING

March 7, 2015

Attend thee, every living thing
to words of godly revelation.
From the earth didst ever spring,
Despite man's gross imagination
all that liveth, everything
alive in earthly habitation.

Thou mightest try, I wouldst propose
with mighty, grandiose entreat,
to find some living thing, one knows
above somewhere, or 'neath thy feet.
That, independent from this earth
of alien ingredient, gives birth,
no such thing grows.

Aha, thou criest with delight,
I have you now, I know of one,
Man doth himself, exception prove.
Not so, broadcasteth my disdain,
thy misconception I remove,
man's element's forever came
from earth, as thou today dost learn,
and do return to earth again.

One resident in earth exists, but
cometh not from earth, I wouldst propose.
He is God's Holy Ghost which liveth
in men's hearts, at least in those
who open up their hearts to Christ.
This gift from God to all men goes,
whilst all who come to true repentance,
Jesus knows.

TIME'S ULTIMATE END

March 5, 2015

I am the true vine, and my Father's the husbandman,
thus spake the Lord to Apostils, attendant.
My Husbandman Father, then purgeth my branches,
that so fruitful a harvest doth flourish resplendent,
whilst thy time on this rotating sphere doth wend,
unto time's ultimate end, Amen,
unto time's oh so ultimate end.

When Jesus explained, as the Father loved me,
even so, have I ever loved you.
Might we then from this lovingness, please be excused,
for this purging doth smack of our being ill used,
whilst our time on this rotating sphere doth wend,
unto time's ultimate end, Amen,
unto time's oh so ultimate end.

While Jesus didst bend to immerse Peter's feet,
Peter self righteously, strongly deterred.
Jesus said, thou knowest not now, but one day thou wilt see,
if I wash thee not now, thou hast no part with me,
whilst thy time on this rotating sphere doth wend,
unto time's ultimate end, Amen,
unto time's oh so ultimate end.

126

Our Lord doth require, ere man's time doth transpire,
that God's tenets, each man must obey.
So to make a good start, receive Christ to thy heart,
do it ere this today's called today,
whilst thy time on this rotating sphere doth wend,
unto time's ultimate end, Amen,
unto time's oh so ultimate end.

WASTE NO TEARS

March 9, 2015

Waste no tears
on my at last, demise.
God's vast sunrise
of sparkling sky
thru ninety years
or so of life
displayed the
light of Christ
upon my oh so
unresponsive heart,
'bout mid stream
of my part
from birth to death.
But my last breath
I pray will find a way
to hopefully display
before the throne of God,
my love for Jesus Christ
as I depart.

EVER LOVING WIVES
March 3, 2015

Ah Memories!
They linger faintly
in the hidden reaches
of an old man's mind.
Recalling love's intensities,
vague, tantalizing memories
old lovers find.

Ah Memories!
How valiantly doth memory
recall, thru misty thoughtfulness
the free, the fanciful remind
of lovely flowers, unknowingly
bestowing all their loveliness
on potential suitors, blind.

Ah Memories!
Sweet years of youthful innocence
when love so carelessly was wasted,
golden chance so casual, tasted
but lacking now, the vested power to bind.
Each flower, eloquently contrives
to tell old men, that thru loves labors lost
they found their ever loving wives,
well worth the cost.

iN MY FATHER'S HOUSE

February 28, 2015

In My Father's house are many mansions,
I go to prepare a place for you.
It is good Lord, to know
that one day when I go,
my house will be ready for me.
In Thy presence a place, within sight of Thy face
for forever's duration to be.

I know You will come to each man, every one
who hideth Thy word in his heart.
Thomas exclaimed, we know not the way,
Jesus told Thomas, I am the Way
if you come not by Me, thru eternity,
God's judgement will set you apart.

I will not leave you comfortless, Jesus exclaimed,
I'll return in a little while.
The world will not see me, but you will, because
I am, I will be and I forever was.
Because I live, this assurance I promise to you,
through eternity's endlessness, you shall live too.

BOB MCCLUSKEY

Meanwhile here on earth, if a man loveth Me,
he will keep my words and my Father will see
that the God Head fully doth come unto him,
and will dwell and remain and that man will begin
to be strengthened by God's Holy Ghost by degree,
as God's Spirit doth teach him all things about Me,
to the Glory Of God The Father.

THIS DAY

February 22, 2015

"CHOOSE YOU THIS DAY,
WHOM YOU WILL SERVE."
Choose Jesus,
God's wonderful name.
For if you do not choose
in the end you will lose,
for then Satan
can make legal claim.

God's Word tells it best,
there is only one way
to join heaven's blest,
don't delay.
God determines "THIS DAY"
for God knoweth man will
everlasting delay,
God knows best.

Consider carefully then
life's cruel destiny, when
man doth carelessly rend
Bible truth.

Bible truth doth portend
where all sinners must end
when God's warning's rejected,
forsooth.
Let's choose Jesus together
my friend.

GOD'S APPOINTING

February 28, 015

How could one know
in the days when Christ walked
amongst men on the earth
that this man was the Christ?
Why, the Father didst show
to His chosen!

Men said, is this not the son
of the very same one
who has walked in our midst
known as Joseph.
Who with Mary his wife
brought this Jesus to life?
Jus' suppose'n!

Thou must earnestly pray
God wouldst mercifully,
in the Spirit this day
with anointing,
bring revelation to thee.
Despite scaled over eyes
allow God to devise
thine appointing!

WHERE WENT THE VOW

October 26, 2014

Where went each thought, that remembereth not
sweet passions from earlier years.
Where went the vow to forget me not,
that she emphasized thru her tears.

Where went the careless intensity,
committed for evermore.
The eternal vow, love's empathy
that didst fade since her last encore.

Was it not in the spring of yesteryear,
that she pledged her eternal love.
She didst ardently swear to be ever near,
troth pledged by the stars above.

Though sixty-odd long years, recedeth now
to the edge of obscurity.
Still, a heart-felt twinge, recalleth the vow
that was never able to be.

Some folk believe, fate doth ever conceive
the twists and turns of romance.
But, could it be God whom we should applaud
for directing our lives, perchance?

UNTRAMMELLED EASE

October 23, 2014

Where might one go
To find untrammelled ease
Surely not thru rain nor snow
It cannot bide
In one of these
I know

Perhaps on farthest shore
Unvisited, alone
Wouldst searcheth for
Contentment there
An idyll prone, to please
For evermore

Oh foolish one, desist
Thy treasure lies
Not in some foreign tryst
But hid within, Christ cries
For thy rebirth to life
In heavens bliss

BOB MCCLUSKEY

WHY DID GOD MAKE MAN
October 22, 2014

Why, do you think, didst God make man,
have you pondered the root of this question.
God is self sufficient, so explain if you can,
to tend to the earth, a suggestion.

Or was it perhaps to give each a new name,
all the animals God had created.
Was the eating of chicken, God's first interdiction,
or was eating no meat over stated.

Did God create all the heavens, including the earth,
just to provide man a place to expand in.
Of the heavenly bodies, was never a dearth
of planets, for mankind to land in.

This, we've bandied about, but I think without doubt
God required many sons to come in.
For His love is expansive, it must be expressed
Upon sons just like Jesus, whose love said it best,
when He went to the cross for our sin.

WHAT TRIGGERS LOVE

October 20, 2014

What are the elements
found in her for him,
or for that matter
found in him for her,
exploding love to then begin

to unconsciously trigger fireworks,
immediately igniting them
to deny unwelcome little quirks
that some would label sin, the jerks,
don't let them in.

Don't come against his lady love,
don't come against her boy.
Onlookers fail to e'er discern
her strategies, his head to turn,
the little tricks she would employ.

But, the eye of the beholder
is where beauty lies, they say.
She and he would then defer
from seeing faults in him or her,
grandeur doth deploy in every way.

BOB MCCLUSKEY

What triggers love, again we ask,
what causes him or her to bask
in unrelenting ecstasy.
A state of being blind we see
as foreign then, to thee and me,
yet brings our hearts to task.

TIME ON MY HANDS

October 17, 2013

Time...as I awake she watcheth me, impatiently,
with hands on hip, pursed lip and tapping toe
observing me.
It may be later than mid morn
when consciousness for me is born,
to once more apprehend her scorn,
reluctantly.

I try to hide but there is not a place
behind which I might neutralize my face,
concealingly.
Time is you see, alert and waiting,
unfailingly ingratiating
my slothfulness anticipating
every morning late, eye-balling me.

Why does not **Time**, her own affairs pursue,
why must she, my contentedness
unfailingly undo.
My day doth start forsooth, quite stark,
then in my mind, **Time's** snide remark
say's action must at once embark
on anything, just something more to do.

But one day, **Time's** come-uppance shall arrive,
when I'll no longer, by her be required
to persevere.
My plan to rest, to never strive,
my friends will cheer, those yet alive
as I escape Old Slue-Foot's jive,
I'm jetting up to Jesus, won't be here.

RiNG THE HEARTS OF MEN

October 16, 2014

What would ring the hearts of men
What is the thing to entrance them when
Into the caverns of thought they flee
For a desperate, new reality
In life

When woefully jaded and filled with fear
As blackened walls of life's end loom near
As they cast about for a reason to try
To lift their carcases e're they die
Once more from the bier

What rapture defied since early youth
When each moment vied to deny the truth
That hovered above in the endless air
Looking down not up, to the glory where
They could live, forsooth

Awake! Awake! To the mystery
God put in place for all men to see
Your ears are deaf, your eyes are blind
Pray God remove the scales, you'll find
Truth will make you free

So, truth in men's hearts is the liberating
Redemptive explosion to make them kings
And priests in the kingdom of God on earth
Without anger or fear, spiritual rebirth
For eternity

COME, LET US RISE

October 6, 2014

Come, let us rise above
the mundane, into rarified
expressions of unsullied love,
where loveliness doth care to bide
with perfection's Holy Dove.

Where selfishness cannot survive
midst pristine perfection, profligate.
Where perfect goodness doth deride
each slightest thought to elevate
the self inside.

Where each, the other doth prefer
in love expressed, divine.
No thought of self endearment
that might enter time
where fear went, clandestine.

Might this dream identify
reality, could it come to birth?
There is a way, I know there is,
I've tasted and can testify,
Christ cancels Satan's every lie
to God enthroned on earth.

LOVE BECKONED
October 8, 2014

Love beckoned, we were young one day
Memory reckons on that far away
Moment, a flash of blinding light
Illuminates as the sun at night
In grand display

Where doth that beauty linger now
Might it yet survive somewhere, somehow
Beauty comes, man's darkness to ignite
For, the darkened need such light
To light our way

We become inured by numbing dregs
To uplifting loveliness that begs
We venture up, redemption draweth nigh
Love expandeth over all the sky
Each lovely day

Love therefor displays in many forms
Lovely maid inspireth lad's reforms
But greatest love that turneth night to day
Is blood of Christ that cleanseth sin away
For evermore

LAST SHEEP SHORN

October 9, 2014

The stage so set, it fashions yet
thru lassitude of time.
A classic ordinance 'tis true,
to everyone, yet one day grew
potentially, divine.

Intended end was yet foregone,
'twould end no other way.
And yet the players stumble on,
before their destiny to fawn
eternity away.

What profit, wouldst our Lord forego
by loosing heart restraints.
These hearts, our Lord didst fashion so,
yet in the fashioning, wouldst know
our petulant complaints.

Each spirit God didst fabricate,
He fashioned with free will.
Free will to either love or hate,
to heav'n or hell ingratiate,
each destiny fulfill.

BOB MCCLUSKEY

God loved each spirit, as He sent
them to their place in life.
He grieved o'er those He didst foreknow,
rebelliously would choose to go
to hell, eternal strife.

This was the price, God chose to pay
for sons like His First Born.
God knew there was no other way,
so patiently has caused delay
till each fractious sheep be shorn.

About the Author

The writer was the product of the depression years in Canada and lacked formal education beyond one and a half years of commercial High School...Bob volunteered for the R.C.A.F. and during basic training and selection at Little Norway in Toronto was discharged because of poor eyesight...Bob then worked one shipping season as fireman on a Great Lakes ship when he received his army conscription notice just as W.W.2 was running down. He completed his army basic training as the war in Europe ended and hoping to yet take part in "The Big Show" he volunteered for the war in the Pacific against Japan...As luck would have it, Japan surrendered just as his army advanced training also ended, leaving a very disappointed Canadian boy at loose ends.

However, optimism was rife back in those days and Bob was off on a variety of jobs over the next few years culminating in a twenty seven year career as manager of retail beer stores for the Brewers Ware-housing Company in Toronto, Ontario. This odyssey was interrupted by a wonderfully dramatic meeting with God's Holy Spirit at the age of fifty while sitting all alone at home early one morning which opened the door to the second half of Bob's life seeking and serving God...Bob joined Dr. Winston Nunes church, Faith Temple in Toronto and served on and chaired his church board...He joined 100 Huntley, daily Christian television at that time and stayed with them as head of Security Counseling Dept. for five years before leaving to join his children's families in Vancouver, B.C.

Surprisingly, at about the age of eighty two and just after the passing of his first wife, Bob started to compose poetry for the first time in his life...This unexpected aberration burst upon him then and has been his consuming passion for the past seven or eight years...We come now to this, his eighth published book of poetry and at his present age, about seven months shy of ninety, common sense would indicate enough already, but one never knows Eh!